Rumble, Rumble

Mark 6:32–44
(Jesus Feeds the Crowd)

by Mary Manz Simon
Illustrated by Dennis Jones

CPH
SAINT LOUIS

Books by Mary Manz Simon
from Concordia Publishing House

Hear Me Read Series

Level 1	Level 2	Big Books
(also available in Spanish)	Daniel & Tattletales	Drip Drop *
Bing!	First Christmas	Follow That Star
Come to Jesus	Hide-and-Seek Prince	Send a Baby
Drip Drop	Hurray for the Lord's Army	Sit Down *
Follow That Star	No-Go King	Too Tall, Too Small
Hide the Baby	Thank You Jesus	What Next?
Hurry, Hurry!	Through the Roof	Where Is Jesus? *
Jibber Jabber	Walk on the Waves	Who Will Help? *
Row the Boat		* also available in Classroom Sets
Rumble, Rumble	**Little Visits Series**	
Send a Baby		
A Silent Night	Little Visits Everyday	
Sit Down	Little Visits for Families	God's Children Pray
Too Tall, Too Small	Little Visits for Toddlers	
Toot! Toot!	Little Visits with God	
What Next?	Little Visits with Jesus	
Where Is Jesus?		
Who Will Help?		
Whoops!		

Copyright © 1990 Concordia Publishing House
3558 S. Jefferson Avenue, St. Louis, MO 63118-3968
Printed in Columbia

6 7 8 9 10 11 12 13 14 15   12 11 10 09 08 07 06 05 04 03

Name

Date

Presented by

To the Adult:

Early readers need two kinds of reading. They need to be read to, and they need to do their own reading. The Hear Me Read Bible Stories series helps you to encourage your child with both kinds.

For example, your child might read this book as you sit together. Listen attentively. Assist gently, if needed. Encourage, be patient, and be very positive about your child's efforts.

Then perhaps you'd like to share the selected Bible story in an easy-to-understand translation or paraphrase.

Using both types of reading gives your child a chance to develop new skills and pride in reading. You share and support your child's excitement.

As a mother and a teacher, I anticipate the joy your child will feel in saying, "Hear me read Bible stories!"

Mary Manz Simon

For Angela Michelle Simon
John 10:27

Here are many people.

Here is Jesus.

The people listen to Jesus.

Many people listen to Jesus.

The people are getting hungry.

Rumble, rumble;

stomachs grumble.

"Food, food," the people say.

Rumble, rumble;

stomachs grumble.

"We are hungry," the people say.

Rumble, rumble;
stomachs grumble.

Jesus said,

"The people want some food."

"Here is some food,"

the people said.

"Here are many, many people,"
said Jesus.

Rumble, rumble;
stomachs grumble.

Jesus said, "Here is some food."

"Here is some food,"

said the people.

"Thank you for the food,"
said the people.

Many, many people
said thank you to Jesus.